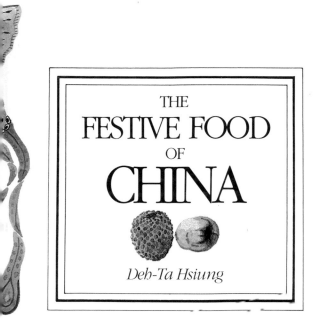

THE
FESTIVE FOOD
OF
CHINA

Deh-Ta Hsiung

ILLUSTRATED BY SALLY MALTBY

SERIES EDITOR: HENRIETTA GREEN

KYLE CATHIE LIMITED

First published 1991 by
Kyle Cathie Limited
20 Vauxhall Bridge Road, London SW1V 2SA

Reprinted 1995

ISBN 1 85626 201 4

A CIP catalogue record for this book is available
from the British Library

Designed and typeset by Geoff Hayes
on his posh new AppleMac

Printed and bound by Chromo Litho, Italy

Recipes are for 4–6 people when served
on their own or 10–12 when combined
with two or three other dishes.

Contents

Little New Year

The festivities for New Year in parts of China start during the last week of the old year – a period known as Little New Year. On the twenty-third or twenty-fourth of the twelfth moon, families gather in front of the Kitchen God, the household's guardian angel. During the rest of the year his statue, picture or tablet lives on the chimney breast, but on this night he is carried into the courtyard by the head of the family and set on fire. This practice sends him to heaven to report on the deeds of his family. Accompanied by the noise of loud firecrackers and with his lips smeared with honey or molasses or sticky sweets to ensure he can only report sweet things or, perhaps, to seal them so that he cannot say anything at all, he is given a great send-off.

Once he has departed, a small feast is served, and feasts and festivities continue for the next seven days, until the grand feast on New Year's Eve. One special dish served during Little New Year is this Chinese version of a fondue.

Chinese Hot Pot

serves 6-8

This is a complete meal in itself. You can find an authentic charcoal or spirit-burning hot pot at most Oriental stores.

450g/1lb lamb fillet (or pork, beef or all), trimmed
225g/8oz chicken breast meat (boned and skinned)
225g/8oz peeled prawns
55g/2oz Chinese dried mushrooms, soaked in warm water for 30–40 minutes
450g/1lb Chinese leaves or spinach
2–3 cakes of bean-curd (*tofu*)
255g/9oz Bean Thread noodles
2litres/3½pints/9cups chicken or meat stock or water

For the dip sauce
100ml/4fl oz/½cup light soy sauce
75ml/5tablespoons/⅓cup dark soy sauce
55g/2oz/¼cup sugar
3–4 spring onions, finely chopped
3–4 slices ginger root, peeled and
    finely chopped
2 garlic cloves, crushed and finely
    chopped (optional)
10ml/2teaspoons sesame seed oil
chilli sauce (optional)

1 Trim the chicken and lamb and cut into wafer-thin slices.

2 Squeeze dry the mushrooms and discard the stalks. Cut the mushrooms, Chinese leaves and bean-curd into small pieces.

3 Soak the noodles for 5–10 minutes until soft.

4 Arrange all the prepared ingredients either on a large plate or on small individual dishes. Arrange the ingredients for the dip sauce on the table ready for mixing by the diners, according to their taste.

5 When you are ready to eat, bring the stock or water to a boil in the hot pot at the table. Each person should then pick up a piece of meat with chopsticks and dip it into the boiling liquid for no more than a few seconds, until the colour of the meat changes – and then quickly dip it in the sauce.

6 When the meats have been eaten, add the vegetables to the pot. Boil for a few minutes, season the liquid with the remaining dip sauce, and serve the soup to finish the meal.

New Year's Eve Grand Feast

New Year's Eve is probably the festival of the year: a time for settling debts in order to start the New Year with a clean slate, and, equally important, a time when all the family gathers together to relax and to enjoy themselves. The Kitchen God is ceremoniously welcomed back with red candles, incense, fire-crackers and offerings of pork, chicken or duck, carp, wine and fruits. The new effigy is placed in its shrine on the chimney breast and then the whole family sits down to a huge feast.

The feast starts with a couple of deep-fried dishes followed by a soup and duck, which is considered special, a leg or hand of pork and, to complete the traditional 'three meats', carp is a must for New Year as it is the fish of good fortune. A bowl or two of vegetables are always served at any Chinese meal with rice, to fill the empty corners.

Butterfly Prawns

For best results, use uncooked king prawns in their shells. Sold headless, they are 8–10cm/3–4in long, and you should get 18–20 prawns per 450g/1lb.

450g/1lb headless king prawns in their shells
20ml/1tablespoon/1½tablespoons light soy sauce
5ml/1teaspoon ground Sichuan pepper
50ml/3tablespoons/¼cup Shao Hsing rice wine or
  dry sherry
10ml/2teaspoons cornflour
2 eggs, lightly beaten
30g/1oz/⅓cup breadcrumbs
about 575ml/1pint/2½cups oil for
  deep-frying
lettuce leaves to garnish
2–3 spring onions, shredded, to garnish

1 Shell the prawns but leave the tails on. Split them in half from the underbelly about three-quarters of the way through, leaving the tails still firmly attached. Marinate in the soy sauce, pepper, wine and cornflour for 10–15 minutes.

2 Pick up a prawn by the tail, dip it in the egg then roll it in the breadcrumbs before lowering it into medium-hot oil. Deep-fry the prawns in batches until golden brown. Remove and drain.

3 To serve, arrange the prawns neatly on a bed of lettuce leaves and garnish with spring onions.

Chicken with Lemon Sauce

550g/1¼lb chicken breast meat
1 or 2 eggs, lightly beaten
60ml/3½tablespoons/¼cup + 2teaspoons cornflour
about 575ml/1pint/3½cups oil for deep-frying
200ml/7fl oz bottled lemon sauce from Oriental
    stores
slices of fresh lemon to garnish

1 Trim the chicken breasts, coat with egg and
cornflour, then deep-fry in hot oil until golden.
Remove and drain.
2 Cut each breast into bite-sized pieces and arrange
on a hot serving plate.
3 Heat about 20ml/1tablespoon/
1½tablespoons oil in a saucepan and
mix in the lemon sauce, blend well
    and pour evenly over the
    chicken. Garnish with lemon
        slices and serve hot.

Eight-treasure Soup

30g/1oz Chinese dried mushrooms soaked for 35–40
  minutes in warm water
30g/1oz dried shrimps soaked for 25–30 minutes in
  warm water
700ml/1¼pints/3cups chicken or meat stock
55g/2oz chicken meat, thinly shredded
55g/2oz pork fillet, thinly shredded
55g/2oz bamboo shoots, thinly shredded
55g/2oz spinach leaves, thinly shredded
1 cake of bean-curd (tofu), sliced
30ml/1½tablespoons/2tablespoons light soy sauce
2 eggs, lightly beaten
20ml/1tablespoon/1½tablespoons cornflour mixed
  with an equal amount of water
salt and pepper to taste
finely chopped spring onion to garnish

1 Squeeze the mushrooms dry, discard stalks and
shred finely. Rinse and drain the shrimps.
2 Bring the stock to a rolling boil, add the shrimps,
chicken, pork and mushrooms, stir to separate, then
add bamboo shoots, bean-curd, spinach and soy
sauce. Bring back to the boil and pour in the eggs.
3 Thicken the soup with the cornflour and water
mixture. Cook for one more minute. Adjust season-
ing and serve hot, garnished with spring onions.

Roast Duck with Stuffing

1 duckling, weighing 2kg/4½lb, cleaned
50ml/3tablespoons/1¼cups dark soy sauce

Stuffing
115g/4oz/½cup glutinous rice or round pudding rice
4–5 medium Chinese dried mushrooms
30g/1oz dried shrimps
giblets (gizzard, heart and liver) of the duck
55g/2oz bamboo shoots
55g/2oz cooked ham
30ml/1½tablespoons/2tablespoons oil
2 spring onions, finely chopped
20ml/1tablespoon/1½tablespoons light soy sauce
20ml/1tablespoon/1½tablespoons Shao Hsing rice
  wine or dry sherry
salt to taste

1 Brush the duck skin with the dark soy sauce.
2 Soak the rice in 175ml/6fl oz/¾cup boiling water
for 20–25 minutes. Soak the dried mushrooms in
warm water for 25–30 minutes, squeeze dry and,
discarding the stalks, cut into pea-sized cubes. Soak
the dried shrimps in warm water for 20 minutes,
rinse and drain. Boil the gizzard gently in water for
10–15 minutes and dice, along with the heart, liver,
bamboo shoots and ham.
3 Heat the oil in a wok and stir-fry the mushrooms,
shrimps, giblets, bamboo shoots, ham and spring
onions for 1 minute. Mix in the light soy sauce and
wine, the rice and its soaking water and salt. Bring to
the boil, then reduce heat and cook for 8–10 minutes, or until all the liquid is absorbed.
4 Pack the stuffing into the duck cavity and close up
the tail opening. Place the duck on a wire rack in a
roasting tin and cook in a preheated 200°C/400°F/
gas6 oven for 30 minutes, then reduce the heat to
180°C/350°F/gas4 and cook for a further 45 minutes.

5 To serve, scrape out the stuffing and spread out on a platter, chop the duck into bite-sized pieces and arrange neatly on top of the stuffing.

Red-cooked Leg or Shoulder of Pork

South of the Yangtze River, where pork is plentiful, this dish is a must for every feast and is the nearest equivalent to the British Sunday joint. Leg of mutton or shin of beef, cut into large chunks, can be cooked this way.

1.35–1.5kg/3–3½lb leg or shoulder of pork, cleaned
4—5 spring onions
3–4 slices of fresh ginger root
50ml/3tablespoons/¼cup light soy sauce
100ml/4fl oz/½cup dark soy sauce
50ml/3tablespoons/¼cup brandy
115g/4oz/½cup rock candy or crystal sugar

1 Make sure the pork skin is free of bristles and score the rind and meat with a few cuts.
2 Place the meat with spring onions and ginger in a large saucepan, skin side down. Cover with cold water and bring to the boil rapidly, skimming constantly. Add the soy sauces and brandy, reduce the heat and simmer, covered, for 30 minutes.
3 Turn the meat over, add the sugar, cover and continue cooking for about 1½ hours. Now reduce the liquor by boiling rapidly, uncovered, for 5–10 minutes.
4 To serve, lift out the meat and place on a deep serving dish, skin side up. Discard the ginger and spring onions and pour the gravy over the pork. The meat should be tender enough to tear into shreds with chopsticks.

Steamed Whole Fish

The last main course of any feast must include a whole fish, because the Chinese word for fish, *yu*, is pronounced the same as the word 'to spare' – and we like to think that there is always something on the table to spare, particularly on New Year's Eve for the start of the New Year.

1 scaled and gutted carp, sea bass, trout or grey
    mullet, weighing about 700g/1⅔lb
5ml/1teaspoon salt
10ml/2teaspoons sesame oil
2–3 spring onions, cut in half lengthways
2 slices fresh ginger root, peeled and finely shredded
30ml/1½tablespoons/2tablespoons light soy sauce
30ml/1½tablespoons/2tablespoons Shao Hsing rice
    wine or dry sherry
20ml/1tablespoon/1½tablespoons oil
finely shredded spring onions to garnish

1 Clean the fish well and dry thoroughly. Score both sides of the fish as far as the bone with diagonal cuts at 1cm/½in intervals. Rub the inside and outside of the fish with salt and sesame oil, then place it on top of the spring onions on a heatproof platter, and place the ginger on top.
2 Put the platter in a hot steamer or inside a wok on a rack, and steam vigorously for 15–18 minutes.
3 Remove the platter from the steamer and pour the soy sauce and wine evenly over the fish; meanwhile, heat the oil until hot, place the shredded spring onions on top of the fish, then pour the hot oil over the whole length of the fish. Serve immediately.

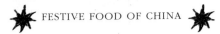
Braised Chinese Vegetables

30g/1oz wood ears (dried black fungus)
225g/8oz Chinese leaves
115g/4oz broccoli or mange-tout
115g/4oz bamboo shoots or carrots
115g/4oz beansprouts or celery hearts
1 small red pepper, cored and deseeded
50ml/3tablespoons/¼cup oil
5ml/1teaspoon salt
5ml/1teaspoon sugar
20ml/1tablespoon/1½tablespoons light soy sauce
sesame oil to garnish

1 Soak the dried fungus in warm water for 10–15 minutes, rinse and drain. Cut the fresh vegetables into a rough dice.

2 Heat the oil in a wok, add the carrots first, if using, followed by broccoli or mange-tout and Chinese leaves about 1 minute later then add the rest of the vegetables and stir-fry for about 2 minutes. Now add salt and sugar, and a little stock or water if necessary. Continue stirring for another minute or so, then add the soy sauce and sesame oil. Serve hot or cold.

New Year's Day

The traditional Chinese calendar is based on the cycles of the moon. The words 'month' and 'moon' are identical because, according to our Chinese lunar calendar, one month equals one moon. The number of days in a month corresponds to the number of days it takes the moon to make one complete revolution around the earth. So some months have twenty-nine days, others thirty days; but the new moon is always on the first of the month and the full moon on the fifteenth day.

New Year's Day is celebrated by children every-where as their birthday. I remember the excitement, the presents, toys and clothes, the little red envelopes I found tucked under my pillow bulging with money.

This is also the day when the gods are honoured with lighted red candles and incense, when food and inscriptions written on red paper are placed in their shrines and everyone wears new clothes. The day starts with a bang of firecrackers to mark the 'Opening the Door to Welcome the Auspicious New Year' ceremony.

Afterwards, throughout the day, people call on each other offering the compliments of the season. They are given tea and the Eight-treasure Box, an octagonal box divided into eight sections containing sweatmeats and nuts. Close relatives and special guests are also offered New Year Cakes or, in the north, *Jiao Zi*, wheat flour dumplings.

New Year Cake

This basic New Year Cake recipe is served with sugar or syrup, but other sweet fillings, all offering different colours and fragrances, include sesame seed paste, red or black bean paste, or honey.

450g/1lb/4cups glutinous rice flour
225g/8oz/1⅓cups brown sugar
about 350ml/12fl oz/1½cups boiling water
30g/1oz lard
oil for frying

1 Sift the flour into a bowl. Dissolve the sugar in the water and slowly add to the flour, mixing to a smooth consistency.
2 Grease a 20cm/8in cake tin with the lard and fill with the dough. Steam over rapidly boiling water for about 2 hours. Remove and invert onto a plate. When cool, refrigerate, well covered, for at least 6–8 hours to harden.
3 To serve, cut the cake into diamond-shaped pieces and shallow-fry in oil on both sides until brown. Serve hot with either caster sugar or golden syrup.

Jiao Zi
(PEKING DUMPLINGS)

Jiao Zi are eaten for breakfast on New Year's Day. Most households make enough to last four or five days, and leave the uncooked *Jiao Zi* outside to freeze in the bitterly cold winter, using them from frozen as required.

Dough
450g/1lb/4cups plain flour
about 450ml/¾pint water
flour for dusting

Filling
450g/1lb Chinese leaves or white cabbage
450g/1lb pork or lamb, minced
3 spring onions, finely chopped
5ml/1teaspoon finely chopped fresh ginger root
10ml/2teaspoons salt
5ml/1teaspoon sugar
30ml/1½tablespoons/2tablespoons light soy sauce
20ml/1tablespoon/1½tablespoons Shao Hsing rice
    wine
10ml/2teaspoons sesame oil

Dip sauce
2–3 slices fresh ginger
    root, finely shredded
60ml/3½tablespoons/
    ¼cup + 2teaspoons
    rice vinegar
30ml/1½tablespoons/
    2tablespoons light
    soy sauce

1 Sift the flour into a bowl, slowly pour in the water and mix to a firm dough. Knead until smooth and soft. Cover with a damp cloth and set aside for 25–30 minutes.

2 Blanch the cabbage leaves until soft; drain and chop finely. Mix in the remaining filling ingredients and blend well.

3 Lightly dust a work surface with flour, knead and roll the dough into a long sausage of about 2.5cm/ 1in diameter. Cut into 80–90 small pieces. Flatten each piece with the palm of your hand, then with a rolling pin roll out each into a pancake about 6cm/ 2½in in diameter.

4 Place about 1 tablespoon of filling in the centre of each pancake and fold it into a half-moon-shaped pouch, then pinch the edges firmly so that the dumpling is tightly sealed.

5 Bring about 2litres/3pints/9cups water to a rolling boil and drop in about 20 dumplings, stirring gently with chopsticks to prevent them sticking together. Cover, bring back to the boil and then add about 150ml/¼pint/⅔cup cold water; bring to the boil again, this time uncovered. Repeat twice more, remove dumplings with a strainer and serve hot with dip sauce. Store any uncooked *Jiao Zi* in the freezer.

Lantern Festival

The Lantern Festival or Big New Year, on the fifteenth day of the first moon, dates from the rule of the Emperor Ming (58–75 AD) of the Han Dynasty, and formally ends the New Year celebrations, marking the return of the spring light and the lengthening of the day.

Lanterns are lit all over the country in homes and temples, and spectacular processions of exquisite silk and paper lanterns in every shape and form take place in the streets; at the end of each procession a magnificent dragon, carried by at least a dozen men, dances to the deafening rhythm of cymbals and drums and firecrackers.

Traditionally, *Tang Yuan*, little round dumplings made of glutinous rice powder, are eaten.

Tang Yuan

These little round dumplings owe their origin to the famous snacks known as *wantons* in the West.

Dough
50g/2oz/½cup sago, soaked for 6 hours in cold water
225g/8oz/2cups glutinous rice flour
about 300ml/½pint/1¼cups cold water

Filling
225g/8oz pork, coarsely minced
pinch of salt
5ml/1teaspoon sugar
20ml/1tablespoon/1½tablespoons light soy sauce
20ml/1tablespoon/1½tablespoons Shao Hsing rice wine
1 spring onion, finely chopped

1 Drain the sago in a sieve for 30 minutes and mix with the glutinous rice flour. Add cold water, knead, and pound to a smooth dough.

2 Mix together all the ingredients for the filling. Set aside for 30–35 minutes.

3 Roll the dough into a long sausage shape, about 2.5cm/1in in diameter, and cut into 1cm/½in pieces. Flatten each piece of dough and place about 2.5ml/½teaspoon of filling in the centre. Carefully draw the edges of dough over the filling, seal and shape into a small ball by rolling between the palms of your hands. The dumplings may be made in advance and refrigerated.

4 For four servings: bring about 700ml/1¼pints/3cups water to a rolling boil, drop in 16 dumplings, one by one, and stir very gently to prevent them from sticking together. Cook vigorously until they all float to the surface, then reduce heat and simmer for 5 minutes. Scoop them into individual bowls and cover with some of the water. Serve hot.

Birthday of Guan Yin

The birthday of the Goddess of Mercy, Guan Yin, is celebrated on the nineteenth day of the second moon.

There are many stories about her origins. In one legend she was the daughter of an Indian prince and a disciple of Gautama, the Buddha. In another she was born in the third century BC as the Chinese daughter of one of the Zhou Emperors and became a nun.

The name 'Guan Yin' also means 'observing or taking note of sounds' and, as such, she is worshipped by both Buddhists and Taoists, appealing primarily to women. They pray to her for prosperity, security and male children. Some devout women even observe a period of fasting – giving up meat, fish, poultry, eggs and dairy products – from the beginning of the second moon until her birthday.

On the dawn of the nineteenth, Guan Yin's shrines are crowded with her followers bringing gifts and food and, although you may find chicken, duck or fish, for the truly devout, vegetarian food is the order of the day.

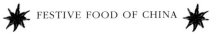

Guan Yin Tang Mein
(VEGETARIAN NOODLES IN SOUP)

This dish owes its origin to Buddhist temples and monasteries, where it would be offered by the monks and nuns to visiting worshippers.

30g/1oz dried bean-curd (tofu) skin
3–4 Chinese dried mushrooms
30g/1oz dried tiger lily buds ('Golden Needles')
55g/2oz water chestnuts
55g/2oz bamboo shoots ⎤ cut into
55g/2oz carrots ⎟ thin strips
55g/2oz spinach or lettuce leaves ⎦
225g/8oz fine noodles (vermicelli)
50ml/3tablespoons/¼cup oil
2.5ml/½teaspoon salt
5ml/1teaspoon sugar
30ml/1½tablespoons/2tablespoons light soy sauce
5ml/1teaspoon sesame oil
thinly shredded spring onions to garnish

1 Soak the bean-curd skin in cold water for 4–6 hours, or in warm water for 2–3 hours, then slice thinly. Soak the mushrooms in warm water for 30–40 minutes, squeeze dry (reserve the water), discard the stalks and cut into thin slices. Soak the lily buds in cold water for 20–30 minutes and rinse until clear.
2 Cook the noodles in boiling water following the instructions on the packet; drain (reserve the water) and place them in a large serving bowl. Pour enough of the cooking liquid into the bowl to half-cover the noodles. Keep warm.
3 Heat the oil in a wok, stir-fry the vegetables for about 2 minutes, add the salt, sugar, soy sauce and a little of the mushroom-soaking water. Bring to boil, add the sesame oil and then pour all the vegetables and liquid over the noodles. Garnish with spring onions and serve hot.

Birthday of the Goddess of the Sea

The birthday of Mazu, the Holy Mother and Goddess of the Sea, is celebrated on the twenty-third day of the third moon. The daughter of a fisherman from Fujian, she is also known as Tian Hou (The Queen of Heaven).

One day when her parents were out fishing, she fell into a trance and saw that they were in grave danger; a storm was raging and their boat was tossing and turning at sea. Rushing down to the beach, she could just see them on the horizon. Fixing her eyes on their tiny boat, she guided them safely back to the shore whilst boats all around were sinking.

From that day, the fishing communities stretching from Fujian in the south east to Taiwan and Hong Kong have prayed to her for protection, for fair weather and a good catch; and there are shrines and temples dedicated to her on every junk and village sea front. On Mazu's birthday the fishermen make pilgrimages to temples dedicated to her in the ports of Fuzhou, Xiamen and Zhaoan.

The daily diet of the fishing folk consists mainly of fish and vegetables, so a festival day offers a rare excuse to eat meat.

Long-braised Pork with Bamboo Shoots

For this popular way of cooking pork and bamboo shoots in south China, the pork should not be too lean, so the bamboo shoots can soak up the excess fat. It can be cooked well in advance and be reheated just before serving.

1kg/2¼lb belly pork
450g/1lb bamboo shoots
30ml/1½tablespoons/2tablespoons oil
50ml/3tablespoons/¼cup light soy sauce
30ml/1½tablespoons/2tablespoons dark soy sauce
50ml/3tablespoons/¼cup Shao Hsing rice wine
20ml/1tablespoon/1½tablespoons sugar
5ml/1teaspoon five-spice powder

1 Cut the pork into 2.5cm/1in cubes. Cut the bamboo shoots into triangular-shaped chunks of the same size.
2 Blanch the pork by immersing in a pan of boiling water and removing as soon as the water starts to boil again. Rinse the pork in cold water and drain.
3 Heat the oil in a large saucepan or pot and stir-fry the pork for about 30 seconds, then add the soy sauces, wine, sugar and just enough water to cover. Bring to the boil, reduce the heat and simmer gently, covered, for 1 hour, turning once or twice.
4 Add the bamboo shoots and five-spice powder, blending well. Cook for another 30 minutes or so under cover. Serve hot.

Qing Ming

Qing Ming means 'pure and clean' and is the name given to the time when families visit and spring clean their relatives' graves in the countryside and bring food and other offerings for the departed.

As *Qing Ming* falls exactly 106 days after the winter solstice, the weather is mild, and after the graves have been tidied and the proper respects paid, most families spoil themselves with a picnic. Only cold food, prepared in advance, is eaten; out of respect for the dead, no fires are lit in the homes for at least two days.

28

'White-cut' Chicken

There are many variations of this famous Cantonese recipe. But whichever version you try, always use a fresh young chicken.

1 young chicken, weighing 1.35kg/3lb
2 spring onions, each tied into a knot
2 slices fresh ginger root, crushed
5ml/1teaspoon Sichuan peppercorns
10ml/2teaspoons salt

Sauce
50ml/3tablespoons/¼cup light soy sauce
30ml/1½tablespoons/2tablespoons Shao Hsing rice wine
5ml/1teaspoon sugar
10ml/2teaspoons sesame oil
5ml/1teaspoon salt

1 Clean the chicken and place in a large pot with enough water to cover. Add the spring onions, ginger and peppercorns; bring to the boil and skim. Add the salt, then cover with a tight-fitting lid and simmer over a low heat for 20–25 minutes.
2 Remove from the heat and leave the chicken to cook gently in the hot liquid, without lifting the lid, for 3–4 hours, or until the liquid is quite cool.
3 To serve, remove the chicken and drain well, reserving the cooking liquid. Either pull the meat off the bone and cut into small pieces, or chop through the bone into bite-sized pieces, then reassemble on a serving dish.
4 Combine the sauce ingredients with about 50ml/ 3tablespoons/¼cup of the cooking liquid and bring to the boil. Pour evenly all over the chicken and serve cold.

Char Siu

These strips of shining red meat are most often seen
hanging in the windows of Chinese restaurants. The
traditional way of cooking *Char Siu* is to skewer the
strips of meat at one end, hook them onto the top
rack of a specially constructed oven and roast them
in suspension. Here is an alternative method for a
domestic oven.

900g/2lb fillet of pork
225g/8oz Hoi Sin (Chinese barbecue) sauce
30ml/1½tablespoons/2tablespoons Shao Hsing rice
   wine or brandy
5ml/1teaspoon sesame oil
30ml/1½tablespoons/2tablespoons honey

1 Cut the pork into strips about 18–20cm/7–8in by
4cm/1½in.
2 Marinate with the Hoi Sin sauce, wine and sesame
oil in a shallow dish under cover for at least 8–12
hours.
3 Place a baking pan filled with about 575ml/1pint/
2½cups boiling water at the bottom of a preheated
220°C/425°F/gas7 oven. Take the pork strips out of
the marinade and drain (reserve the marinade). Place
the meat flat on a wire rack and roast on the top
shelf of the oven for 15–20 minutes, allowing the
juices to drip into the pan of water. Baste with the
marinade, reduce the oven temperature to 180°C/
350°F/gas4, and continue roasting for a further 20–25
minutes.
4 Remove the meat from the oven and brush with
the honey (thinned down with a little water); then
return the meat to the oven and cook for another
4–5 minutes to crisp the outside a little and give it a
rich colour.

5 When the meat is quite cool, slice it across the grain just before serving; this preserves the flavour and moist texture. Bring the marinade to a boil with the drippings and water in the baking pan; simmer gently for a few minutes and strain into a jug to serve with the meat.

Soy-braised Duck

1 duck, weighing 2kg/4½lb
10ml/2teaspoons salt
1.1litres/2pints/5cups water
3–4 star anise
2 cinnamon sticks
5ml/1teaspoon Sichuan peppercorns
2–3 spring onions, each tied into a knot
3–4 slices of fresh ginger root, crushed
115g/4oz/½cup rock candy or crystal sugar
50ml/3tablespoons/¼cup Shao Hsing rice wine or
  brandy
75ml/5tablespoons/⅓cup light soy sauce
50ml/3tablespoons/¼cup dark soy sauce

1 Clean the duck well, then blanch in boiling water.
Remove and rinse in cold water, and rub the cavity
with the salt.
2 Bring the water with all the remaining
ingredients to the boil, add the
duck, breast side down, bring back
to the boil, then reduce the heat
and simmer under cover for 20
minutes; turn the bird over and
cook, still under cover, for a
further 20 minutes.
3 Turn off the heat and let the
bird cool in the liquid, without
lifting the lid for at least 3–4 hours.
4 To serve, remove the
duck and drain. Chop into
small bite-sized pieces and use
a little of the strained
liquid as a sauce.

Baked Whole Fish

Salmon or turbot steaks can also be used for this recipe.

1 scaled and gutted carp, sea bass, trout or grey
    mullet, weighing about 700g/1⅔lb
2.5ml/½teaspoon salt
5ml/1teaspoon sesame oil
2–3 spring onions, finely shredded
2–3 slices fresh ginger root, finely shredded
20ml/1tablespoon/1½tablespoons crushed black
    beans
20ml/1tablespoon/1½tablespoons light soy sauce
20ml/1tablespoon/1½tablespoons Shao Hsing rice
    wine
coriander leaves to garnish

1 Clean and dry the fish well. Score both sides as far as the bone with diagonal cuts at 1cm/½in intervals, and rub the inside with the salt (this process is unnecessary if cooking fish steaks instead of a whole fish).
2 Grease a double folded large sheet of aluminium foil with the sesame oil and place the fish on top of a few strips of spring onions and ginger root; mix the crushed black beans with the soy sauce and wine,   spread out evenly all over the fish, and then add the rest of the spring onions and ginger root. Fold and double-fold the edges of the aluminium foil to form a loose parcel, pinching together the edges so that liquids will not run out.
3 Cook the fish in a preheated 200°C/400°F/gas6 oven for 25–30 minutes.
4 To serve, unwrap the parcel carefully when cool and garnish with coriander leaves.

Fried Rice

350g/12oz/1¼cups long-grain rice
450ml/¾pint cold water
10ml/2teaspoons salt
115g/4oz cooked and peeled prawns
115g/4oz cooked ham
3–4 eggs
2–3 spring onions, finely chopped
115g/4oz green peas
50ml/3tablespoons/¼cup oil

1 Place the rice in a saucepan with the water and a pinch of salt, bring to the boil and stir once to prevent it sticking to the bottom of the pan. Reduce the heat to very low, cover with a tight-fitting lid and cook for 15 minutes. Fluff the rice up with a fork or spoon then leave to cool until hard.
2 Pat dry the prawns and cut the ham into small pea-sized cubes. Beat the eggs with a pinch of salt and a few bits of the finely chopped spring onions.
3 Heat the oil in a wok and lightly scramble the eggs; add the prawns, ham and peas, stir-fry for about 1 minute, and then add the rice with the remaining salt and spring onions. Blend well, stirring to separate each grain. Serve hot or cold.

Sponge Cake

Traditionally, this cake is made with nine layers, each layer a different colour. Here is a simplified version of a single, one-colour layer.

4 eggs
115g/4oz/½cup caster sugar
100ml/4fl oz/½cup milk
225g/8oz/2cups self-raising flour
2.5ml/½teaspoon bicarbonate of soda
pinch of salt
30g/1oz lard
50ml/3tablespoons/¼cup vegetable oil

1 Beat the eggs in a bowl. Add the sugar and continue beating until the mixture is thick and pale in colour. Stir in the milk. Sift together the flour, soda and salt and fold into the egg mixture.
2 Melt the lard and allow to cool, then mix with the oil. Gently stir into the egg mixture. Pour into a greased 20cm/8in round cake tin and steam for 20 minutes. Remove the cake from the tin while still hot and cool on a rack.
3 Cut the cake into 6–8 wedges and serve.

Dragon Boat Festival

On the fifth day of the fifth moon, dragon boat races are held all over China, when long paddle-boats, garishly decorated as dragons, compete against each other to commemorate the anniversary of Chu Yuan's death.

An honest, upright poet-statesman full of integrity, Chu Yuan drowned himself in the river Miluo Jiang in Hunan province in 295 BC in protest against the corruption of the government. The people were so upset that they took to their boats to search for his body. They threw rice and eggs into the water in an attempt to draw away the fishes, hoping the fish would prefer to nibble them rather than Chu Yuan's mortal remains. As a reminder people still eat *Zong Zi*, a form of dumpling made of glutinous rice wrapped in bamboo leaves, and salted eggs.

Zong Zi

(GLUTINOUS RICE WRAPPED IN BAMBOO LEAVES)

From the wide range of different fillings for *Zong Zi*, here are two, one sweet and one savoury.

Sweet filling for 12 Zong Zi
900g/2lb/4cups glutinous rice
20ml/1tablespoon/1½tablespoons oil
450g/1lb sweet black bean paste

1 Soak the rice for 2 hours, drain, change the water and soak for a further 30 minutes. Drain well, then mix in the oil.
2 Roll the black bean paste into a sausage about 2.5cm/1in in diameter. Cut into 12 sections, and flatten each slightly.

Savoury filling for 12 Zong Zi
450g/1lb/2cups glutinous rice
75ml/5tablespoons/⅓cup oil
5ml/1teaspoon salt
6–8 Chinese dried mushrooms
225g/8oz dried chestnuts
30ml/1½tablespoons/
   2tablespoons dried
   shrimps
285–350g/10–12oz *Char
   Siu* pork, or ham
2–3 salted duck egg yolks,
   or hardboiled egg yolks
2.5ml/½teaspoon sugar
20ml/1tablespoon/1½tablespoons Shao Hsing rice
   wine
20ml/1tablespoon/1½tablespoons light soy sauce
30ml/1½tablespoons/2tablespoons finely chopped
   spring onions

1 Soak the rice for 2 hours, drain and change water.
Soak for a further 30 minutes, then drain well. Mix
with about one third of the oil and half the salt.
2 Soak the dried mushrooms in warm water for
20–25 minutes, the dried chestnuts for 25–30 minutes, and the dried shrimps for 20 minutes. Squeeze
dry the mushrooms, discard the stalks, then cut into
small cubes the same size as the shrimps. Peel the
chestnuts and dice with the pork or ham. Rinse and
drain the shrimps. Chop the egg yolks and set aside.
3 Heat the remaining oil in a wok, stir-fry all the
ingredients except the egg yolks, add the seasonings
and spring onions and blend well. Set aside.

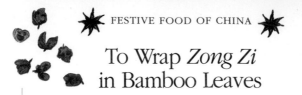

To Wrap *Zong Zi* in Bamboo Leaves

48 dried bamboo leaves
24 strings, each about 1.5m/1½yd long

1 Soak the bamboo leaves in warm water for 2–3 hours, rinse in fresh water then drain and wipe dry.
2 Place two leaves side by side, slightly overlapping; fold the two bottoms over together to form a triangular pouch. Add a portion of the rice and place a piece of the bean paste on the rice if making sweet *Zong Zi*; or place some of the savoury filling with a few bits of the chopped egg yolks if making savoury *Zong Zi*. Cover the filling with more rice and fold the leaves over the top and round the pouch to produce a plump, triangular-shaped bundle. Tie securely with string. Leave a little leeway when wrapping up the bundle, as the rice will expand during cooking.
3 To cook, bring a large pot or wok of water to a rolling boil, drop in the *Zong Zi* and simmer gently for 2–3 hours. Cook the sweet and savoury *Zong Zi* in separate pots.
4 To serve, open the *Zong Zi* packages at the table and serve hot. Extra sugar may be required for the sweet ones, and salt and pepper for the savoury ones. Any left-overs can be reheated, but they must be unwrapped; they usually taste even better than the first time.

Five-spice Tea Eggs

The egg represents fertility and its round smooth shape symbolises good luck and happiness. It also features prominently in many of the Chinese festivals as an offering to the Gods. According to legend, when the world began the universe was egg-shaped, the yolk representing the earth and the white the heavens. Then Pan-ku, primal man, separated them and the bright and clear element – yang – became heaven and the dark and murky yin formed the earth.

12 eggs
5ml/1teaspoon salt
50ml/3tablespoons/¼cup light or dark soy sauce
2–3 star anise, or 5ml/1teaspoon five-spice powder
50ml/3tablespoons/¼cup black China tea leaves

1 Hardboil the eggs for 6–8 minutes. Drain and tap the shells gently with a spoon or roll the eggs on a hard surface until they are cracked finely all over.
2 Put the eggs back in the saucepan, cover with fresh water, add the salt, soy sauce, spice and tea leaves. Bring to the boil and simmer for about 45–50 minutes. Allow the eggs to cool in the liquid.
3 To serve, shell the eggs to reveal a beautiful marbled pattern.

The Lotus Festival

The Lotus Festival is celebrated on the twenty-fourth day of the sixth moon. It also coincides with the coming of the summer rains when the parched earth is revitalized and the ripening crops receive much-needed moisture.

The red lotus *(Nelumbium speciosum)* grows in lakes, ponds and marshes and is particularly beautiful after a shower as drops of water collect at the base of its jade-green leaves and shine like diamonds in the sun. No wonder the crowds row in little boats to admire the sumptuous pink flowers.

Flowers have always been used by artists throughout China to represent the four seasons: the summer flower is the lotus blossom, for autumn the chrysanthemum, for winter plum blossom, and for spring the peony.

The lotus blossom is also closely associated with Buddha. The essence of the Buddhist doctrine is universal redemption and the lotus has come to symbolize man raising himself above the material world to realize his divine nature – for although the lotus grows in mud, it emerges in gorgeous splendour in full bloom.

Its roots, fruits and leaves are all edible; sliced fresh roots are added to stir-fried vegetables, dried leaves are mainly used for wrapping, the seeds, which have medicinal value, make one of the best sweetmeats, and the kernels or lotus-nuts are boiled in soup, roasted or eaten raw.

Steamed Pork with Ground Rice

Traditionally the pork is steamed on a bed of lotus leaves in a bamboo steamer. But here is an alternative method.

675g/1½lb belly pork, boned but with skin on
2.5ml/½teaspoon salt
30ml/1½tablespoons/2tablespoons light soy sauce
5ml/1teaspoon sugar
20ml/1tablespoon/1½tablespoons Shao Hsing rice wine
115g/4oz/½cup ground rice
1-2 star anise

1 Cut the pork into 5cm/2in by 8cm/3in slices and marinate with the salt, soy sauce, sugar and wine for 20–25 minutes.
2 Brown the rice and star anise in a wok or frying pan over medium heat until golden, remove and crush with a rolling pin until fine. Coat each piece of pork with the ground rice, pressing it in well.
3 Arrange the pork in one layer, skin side down, in a bowl or dish. Steam vigorously for at least 4–5 hours, or until the meat is very tender.
4 To serve, turn the meat onto a dish so that the skin side faces up. Serve hot with additional seasonings such as soy sauce and chilli sauce.

Double Seventh Festival

On the seventh day of the seventh moon, unmarried girls celebrate the Double Seventh Festival by making offerings to the Weaver Maid.

Ancient folklore has it that once upon a time Cowherd the orphan was banished into the wilderness by his wicked sister-in-law. All he was allowed to take with him was an old buffalo that he had once rescued from starvation. The buffalo turned into a Fairy Godmother and produced a magic bean that grew up into the skies. Cowherd climbed the stalk and when he reached the heavens discovered the King and Queen's seven daughters bathing in the celestial pool.

On the instructions of the Fairy Godmother he ran off with the clothes of Weaver Maid, daughter number seven, and the prettiest of all. She was forced to descend to earth to retrieve her modesty, and once there found herself in such a compromising position that she had no choice but to marry Cowherd.

During three very happy years she bore Cowherd twins, and taught the earth maidens how to weave silk and to embroider, but her parents decided that it was high time she returned to the fold before she was too corrupted by earthly pleasure and so her mother came down to earth and dragged her away. Cowherd and the twins ran after her and almost caught up with her, but the Queen drew a line across the heaven with a stroke of her silver pin and formed the Celestial River or Milky Way to separate the lovers for ever. The King, moved by the sound of their weeping, took pity on them and consented to allow them to be reunited once a year on the Double Seventh.

On this night the magpies flock together to form a bridge with their wings over the Milky Way and young girls offer gifts of watermelon, luscious fruit and sweetmeats and, in return, beg the Weaver Maid for help and guidance in their needlework.

Fruit Salad in Watermelon

Seven different fruits are used for this Double Seventh Festival recipe.

225g/8oz/1cup rock candy or crystal sugar (optional)
575ml/1pint/2½cups water (optional)
1 small watermelon
6 fruits from the following: pineapple, pears, grapes, lychees, tangerines, peaches, banana, cherries, papaya, mango, kiwi fruit

1 If no canned fruit with syrup is used, dissolve the rock candy in boiling water, then cool.
2 Slice about 5cm/2in off the top of the watermelon and scoop out the flesh, discarding the seeds; cut the flesh into small chunks. Prepare other fresh fruits by cutting them into small chunks.
3 Fill the watermelon shell with fruits and syrup. Chill and serve cold.

Festival of Hungry Ghosts

The Festival of the Hungry Ghosts dates from the first century AD, when Buddhism was first introduced to China. It is held on the fifteenth day of the seventh moon in honour of the unhappy dead or 'orphaned spirits' – those who have died far from home, or have drowned, or have neither marked grave nor descendants to perpetuate their memory.

Vegetarian food, in the Buddhist tradition, is offered to the hungry ghosts to assuage their pangs and gain their gratitude, for unless they are pacified by food they seek living substitutes. It is also customary to burn paper clothing and money to appease the spirits and, in some parts of China, lanterns are lit to help wandering ghosts find their way.

Ten-variety Vegetables

The Chinese never mix ingredients indiscriminately, but select carefully to achieve a harmonious balance of colour, aroma, flavour and texture.

4–6 Chinese dried mushrooms, soaked for 30–40 minutes in warm water
1 cake bean-curd (tofu)
55g/2oz mange-tout or French beans
125g/4oz each of Chinese leaves, cauliflower, courgettes, carrots, white mushrooms, fresh beansprouts
55g/2oz water chestnuts
60ml/3½tablespoons/¼cup + 2teaspoons oil
5ml/1teaspoon salt
5ml/1teaspoon sugar
30ml/1½tablespoons/2tablespoons light soy sauce
5ml/1teaspoon sesame oil

1 Squeeze dry the mushrooms, reserving the water, and discard the stalks; half or quarter them according to their size.
2 Cut the bean-curd into about 12 small pieces, then harden the pieces in a pot of lightly salted boiling water for 2–3 minutes. Remove and drain.
3 Top and tail the mange-tout or French beans; leave whole if small, snap in half if large. Cut the other vegetables into a roughly uniform size, except the beansprouts, which need only be washed and rinsed.
4 Heat about half the oil in a flameproof casserole or saucepan and lightly brown the bean-curd pieces on both sides. Remove with a slotted spoon and set aside.
5 Heat the remaining oil and stir-fry the rest of the vegetables for about 2 minutes, then add the bean-curd with the salt, sugar, soy sauce and a little of the mushroom-soaking water; stir to blend well, cover, reduce the heat and simmer for 4–5 minutes.

The Mid-autumn Festival

Around the time of the autumnal equinox, on the fifteenth day of the eighth moon, there is the Mid-autumn or Moon Festival.

Yue Lao, the 'Old Man in the Moon' is also the universal match-maker. This is the night when he and his little white rabbit helper are busily engaged binding couples together with invisible red silk thread. According to an old saying the mid-autumn moon always shines extra brightly as 'the sky is high and the weather crisp and fine' and everyone celebrates with gifts of fruit, sweets and, of course, moon cakes.

Moon Cakes

During the Mongol rule in China in 1271–1368 guards were billeted in every household to watch for signs of uprising. The Chinese, however, would not be suppressed. By sending hidden messages hidden inside moon cakes they were able to plot and scheme to overthrow the invaders.

Moon Cakes are golden brown pastry pies enclosing any number of fillings to suit all pockets and tastes and stamped on top with the emblem of the deity.

Moon Cakes Home Style

Pastry A
285g/10oz/2½cups flour
170g/6oz lard or shortening, softened
about 150ml/¼pint/⅔cup water
10ml/2teaspoons sugar
pinch of salt

Pastry B
170g/6oz/1½cups flour
170g/6oz lard or shortening, softened

Filling
450g/1lb sweet red bean paste

1 Sift the flour for pastry A into a mixing bowl and add the lard and water. Slowly work in and add the sugar and salt. Knead until smooth.

2 Sift the flour for pastry B into another bowl. Add the lard. Work in and knead until smooth. On a lightly dusted surface, roll the two doughs into two 'sausages', then divide each into 24 portions.

3 Roll each portion into a round ball and flatten with a rolling pin, making the pastry A circles larger than those of B. Place pastry B circles on top of the A circles. Fold four edges of the A over the B pastry to form a square, and gently roll out into a rectangular shape. Fold the two ends into the centre to form a square again, then lightly roll out into a circular shape, fairly thin.

4 When all the pastry cases are made, divide the red bean paste into 24 portions and roll each into a small ball, then flatten slightly. Place one in the centre of each circle of pastry and pull the edges together to enclose the paste. Brush with a little water or beaten egg if the edges do not stick well.

5 To cook, place the cakes on a greased and floured baking tray. Bake in a preheated 200°C/ 400°F/gas6 oven for about 20 minutes. Remove and serve cold.

Double Ninth Festival

The ninth day of the ninth moon is celebrated as the Double Ninth Festival throughout China. It is also known as the Festival of Mounting the Heights (*deng kao*), and it is considered lucky to climb to a high place to take in the clear, fresh air. Kite flying is a popular spectacle on the hilltops on this day; and since almost all ancestral tombs are on the high grounds the people take this opportunity to pay a visit and clear the summer growth from the graves. Sacrifices are offered, after which worshippers picnic in the open, as they did for the *Qing Ming* Festival.

Five-spiced Spare Ribs

Spices in Chinese food almost certainly have religious connections, cleansing the body and purifying the soul.

1kg/2¼lb pork, lamb or veal spare ribs

Marinade
20ml/1tablespoon/1½tablespoons sugar
30ml/1½tablespoons/2tablespoons light soy sauce
2 garlic cloves, crushed
50ml/3tablespoons/¼cup Shao Hsing rice wine or brandy
10ml/2teaspoons five-spice powder
75ml/5tablespoons/⅓cup Hoi Sin (Chinese barbecue) sauce

1 Trim off any excess fat from the ribs and cut into individual pieces. Combine the marinade ingredients

and pour over the ribs in a baking dish; marinate for
2–3 hours, turning occasionally.

2 Roast in a preheated 230°C/450°F/gas8 oven for
15 minutes, then add a little water (about 100ml/
4fl oz/½cup) and reduce the heat to 200°C/400°F/
gas6; cook for another 30–35 minutes, turning once
or twice. Serve hot or cold

Drunken Chicken

Be sure to use a young chicken for this; never use a
frozen chicken or an old broiler.

1 young chicken, weighing 1.35kg/3lb
2litres/3½pints/9cups water
20ml/1tablespoon/1½tablespoons salt
2–3 spring onions, cut into short lengths
3–4 slices peeled ginger root
10ml/2teaspoons Sichuan peppercorns
3–4 star anise
50ml/3tablespoons/¼cup Shao Hsing rice wine
100ml/4fl oz/½cup Gao Liang (sorghum) spirit,
    brandy or whisky

1 Clean the chicken well, then blanch in a pot of
boiling water for 2–3 minutes. Remove and rinse in
cold water.

2 Bring the water to the boil with the salt, spring
onions, ginger, Sichuan peppercorns, star anise and
rice wine. Place the chicken in the liquid, reduce
heat and simmer the bird under cover for 35–40
minutes; leave to cool.

3 Joint the chicken into four quarters. Strain the
liquid, mix with the spirit and pour over the chicken
pieces; leave to marinate under cover for 5–6 hours.

4 To serve, chop the chicken into bite-sized pieces,
pour over a little of the marinade and serve cold.

Cold Tossed Noodles

55g/2oz dried shrimps
50ml/3tablespoons/¼cup Shao Hsing rice wine
350g/12oz egg noodles
20ml/1tablespoon/1½tablespoons oil
170g/6oz fresh beansprouts
3–4 slices ginger root, thinly shredded
50ml/3tablespoons/¼cup light soy sauce
30ml/1½tablespoons/2tablespoons vinegar
10ml/2teaspoons sugar
5ml/1teaspoon red chilli oil (optional)
finely shredded spring onions to garnish
5ml/1teaspoon sesame oil, to garnish

1 Soak the dried shrimps in hot water for 5 minutes, rinse and drain, then coarsely chop and marinate in the rice wine for 15 minutes.
2 Cook the noodles in a pan of boiling water following the instructions on the packet. Rinse in cold water and drain, then add the oil and mix well.
3 Blanch the beansprouts, then rinse in cold water. Drain and set aside.
4 Gently heat the shredded ginger, soy sauce, vinegar, sugar and chilli oil with a little water to make a sauce.
5 To serve, spread the noodles on a large serving dish. Sprinkle over the beansprouts, the chopped shrimps and wine, shredded spring onions and sesame oil. Finally, pour over the sauce, toss and serve.

Crab with Spring Onions and Ginger

2 medium-sized crabs, each weighing about
   400g/14oz
60ml/3½tablespoons/¼cup + 2teaspoons oil
3–4 spring onions, finely chopped

4–5 slices   ginger root, finely chopped
2.5ml/½teaspoon salt
20ml/1tablespoon/1½tablespoons sugar
30ml/1½tablespoons/2tablespoons Shao Hsing rice
   wine
30ml/1½tablespoons/2tablespoons light soy sauce
20ml/1tablespoon/1½tablespoons vinegar
10ml/2teaspoons cornflour blended with an equal
   amount of cold water
coriander leaves to garnish

1 Break off the legs and crack the claws of the
crabs. Wash off any mud and green matter both
outside and inside the shell, and discard the feathery
gills and the sac. Break the body into two or three
pieces.
2 Heat the oil in a wok and fry the crab pieces until
golden. Remove and drain.
3 Add the spring onions and ginger to what is left of
the oil in the wok; add the salt, sugar, wine, soy
sauce, vinegar and a little stock or water. Bring to
the boil, return the crab pieces to be coated by the
sauce. Braise for 2–3 minutes, then thicken the sauce
with the cornflour-and-water mixture; blend well.
Serve hot or cold garnished with coriander leaves.

Birthday of the City Gods

The twenty-fifth day of the ninth moon is the anniversary of the City Gods, whose duties are to care for the souls of their dead parishioners and ward off epidemics and disasters. Every walled town in China would have at least one temple built specially for their patron saints, and during this important religious festival crowds would gather in the temple compounds, and stalls and stands selling all kinds of commodity would be set up. The highlight would be a parade through the town, with colourful floats, tableaux, firecrackers and music.

Though no particular dish would have been eaten during this period, the following recipe is one of the best items sold by the street vendors.

Crispy Vegetarian Spring Rolls

1 packet of 20 frozen spring roll skins
225g/8oz fresh beansprouts
115g/4oz each of tender leeks or spring onions, carrots, bamboo shoots, white mushrooms
about 575ml/1pint/2½cups oil for deep-frying
5ml/1teaspoon each of salt and sugar
20ml/1tablespoon/1½tablespoons light soy sauce
20ml/1tablespoon/1½tablespoons Shao Hsing rice wine (optional)
20ml/1tablespoon/1½tablespoons plain flour mixed with equal amount of water

1 Take the spring roll skins out of the packet and defrost thoroughly.
2 Wash and rinse the beansprouts in cold water, discard the husks and drain. Shred all the vegetables to roughly the same size as the beansprouts.

3 Heat about 50ml/3tablespoons/¼cup of the oil in a wok or frying-pan, stir-fry the vegetables for about 1 minute, then add the salt, sugar, soy sauce and wine (if using), and continue cooking for a further 1–1½ minutes, stirring continuously. Remove and leave to cool.

4 To make the spring rolls: cut each spring roll skin in half diagonally, and, with the triangle pointing away from you, place one teaspoon of the vegetables about a third of the way down the skin, lift the lower flap over the filling and roll once, then fold over both ends and roll once more. Brush the upper edge with a little flour-and-water paste, and roll into a neat package. Repeat until all the filling is used up. Lightly dust a tray with flour and place the spring rolls in rows with the flap side down. (They can be kept in the refrigerator for a day or two, or they can be frozen for up to six months.)

5 To cook, heat the oil until smoking, then reduce the heat or even turn it off for a while. Deep-fry the spring rolls 6–8 at a time for 3–4 minutes, or until golden and crispy; remove and drain. Increase the heat to high again before frying the next batch.

6 Serve hot with a dip sauce such as soy sauce, vinegar, chilli sauce or salt and pepper, etc.

Toffee Water Chestnuts

Fresh water chestnuts (as opposed to canned ones)
are available during the late autumn and winter
months in the Chinatown districts of both the United
States and Britain.

450g/1lb water chestnuts
10–12 bamboo skewers (satay sticks), soaked in
 water for 25–30 minutes
20ml/1tablespoon/1½tablespoons oil
115g/4oz/½cup caster sugar
50ml/3tablespoons/¼cup fruit syrup
about 20ml/1tablespoon/1½tablespoons hot water

1 Wash and scrape the water chestnuts but do not
peel. Boil in a pan of water for 4–5 minutes, then
remove and drain. (If using canned water chestnuts,
they are already peeled and cooked, so just rinse and
drain.) Thread about 6–8 water chestnuts onto each
bamboo stick.
2 Heat the oil in a frying pan, add the sugar, syrup
and water. Bring to the boil, then reduce the heat
and stir until the sugar is caramelized. Add the
skewers and turn until the water chestnuts are
covered all over with the toffee. Serve hot or cold.

Festival of the Winter Solstice

The chief festival during the eleventh moon is the Winter Solstice or *Dong Zhi*. It marks the turning point of the year – the passing of the shortest day – and the dying year also evokes memories of the dead. The Chinese believe that ghosts are much busier during the longest night so great preparations are made for their visit.

A lavish feast is laid out before the ancestral altar, empty chairs for the spirits are set at the head of the table and they are invited to join in the feast. After a few moments of respectful silence the living members of the household all sit down and tuck in.

Eight-treasure Rice Pudding

Eight-treasure Rice Pudding corresponds to the English Christmas pudding as a national dish, and it is traditionally made by a new bride who has married into the family during the year. The Chinese are delightfully vague about the pudding's eight treasures, which might include different kinds of sugar and whole grains (never meal or flour), beans, dates, nuts and fruits.

225g/8oz/1cup glutinous rice
300ml/½pint/1¼cups water
30ml/1½tablespoons/2tablespoons sugar
115g/4oz/¾cup lard
15 dried red dates (jujubes), pitted
30 raisins
20 almond splits, chopped
10 candied cherries
10 pieces angelica, chopped
225g/8oz red bean paste

Syrup
50g/2oz/¼cup sugar
150ml/¼pint/⅔cup water
10ml/2teaspoons cornflour blended with equal
    amount of water

1 Bring the water and rice to the boil, reduce the
heat, cover and cook for 10–15 minutes, or until the
water is absorbed. Add sugar and about half the lard.
Mix well.
2 Brush a 900ml/1⅔pint/4cup capacity mould or
pudding basin with the remaining lard. Cover the
bottom and sides with a thin layer of the rice
mixture. Gently press a layer of the fruit and nuts,
attractively arranged in neat rows, into the rice so
they will show when the pudding is turned out.
3 Cover the fruit and nuts with another layer of rice,
much thicker this time. Fill the centre with the red
bean paste and cover with the remaining rice. Press
gently to flatten the top. Cover with greaseproof
paper or aluminium foil.
4 Steam the pudding for 1 hour. A few minutes
before serving, make the syrup: dissolve the sugar in
the water in a small saucepan, bring to the boil and
stir in the cornflour and
water mixture; simmer
gently, stirring, until
thickened.
5 To serve, invert the
pudding onto a
warmed plate. Pour
over the syrup and
serve immediately.

The Sacrificial Moon

The Sacrificial or twelfth moon is known as *la yue*. This is the time of year for 'sweeping the house', re-lacquering the front gates in vermillion red (the colour for good luck and rejoicing) and whitewashing the outer walls and re-papering the windows.

The eighth day is celebrated as a preliminary New Year Festival with a thick porridge called *La ba zhou* for breakfast. Made from cereals – millet, wheat, sorghum, corn and several kinds of rice – and lentils, nuts and dried fruit, it is first offered to the Ancestral Tablets before being eaten by the family. Sometimes a bowl is sent as a gift to friends or family, in which case it has to arrive before the first stroke of noon.

This is also when the laying in of provisions for the New Year starts. Cured meat such as bacon, sausages or duck are made in great quantities and hung up outside to dry in the winter sun.

Pork Sausages

These strings of rosy sausages seen hanging in the
windows of Chinese restaurants are akin to the
continental salami or saucisson.

675g/1½lb lean pork
225g/8oz pork fat
20ml/1tablespoon/1½tablespoons salt
30ml/1½tablespoons/2tablespoons sugar
5ml/1teaspoon five-spice powder
30ml/1½tablespoons/2tablespoons light or dark soy
    sauce
150ml/¼pint/⅔cup Shao Hsing rice wine or brandy
about 3m/10ft sausage (chipolata size) casing
22 strings, each about 10cm/4in long

1 Coarsely chop the pork and fat and marinate with
the salt, sugar, spice, soy sauce and wine for at least
8 hours or overnight.
2 Carefully attach the casing to the end of a funnel,
and tie the other end of the casing with string Push
the meat mixture into the casing through the funnel
and squeeze to distribute the meat evenly throughout. The sausage should be loosely packed. Once all
the meat has been stuffed into the casing, tie off the
funnel end. Tie the casing at 15cm/6in intervals and
prick the sausage all over with a fine pin.
3 Hang the sausage in an airy place to dry for at
least 3–4 days, or the process can be hastened by
using a fan heater for 24–36 hours.
4 When completely dry, store the sausages in the
refrigerator; they will keep for weeks if wrapped
airtight, and up to six months in the freezer.
5 To serve, cut into thin diagonal slices and fry in a
little oil until the fat bits turn translucent; or, better
still, steam on top of rice for 10–15 minutes.

Pickled Vegetables

Green vegetables are in short supply at this time of the year, so any surplus is pickled or preserved for the long winter months.

225–285g/8–10oz each of any five of the following:
  radish or turnip, carrot, Chinese leaves, green and/
  or white cabbage, cauliflower, celery, onion, leek,
  spring onion (white parts only), garlic cloves
2.25litres/2quarts/10½cups water, boiled and cooled
115g/4oz/½cup salt
55g/2oz chilli peppers
30g/1oz Sichuan peppercorns
115g/4oz fresh ginger root, peeled and sliced
115g/4oz/½cup sugar
150ml/¼pint/⅔cups Chinese distilled spirit, or
  brandy, rum, whisky, etc.

1 Put the water into a large, clean earthenware or glass jar. Add the salt, chillies, peppercorns, ginger, sugar and spirit.
2 Wash and trim the vegetables, peel if necessary and dry well. Put them into the jar and seal it, making sure it is airtight. Place the jar in a cool place and leave the vegetables to pickle for at least five to six days before serving.
3 Use a pair of clean chopsticks or tongs to pick the vegetables out of the jar. Do not allow any grease to enter the jar. You can replenish the vegetables, adding a little more salt each time. If a white scum appears on the surface of the brine, add a little more sugar and spirit. The longer the pickling lasts, the better the taste.